Trek Alongside the Mighty Packs of
WOLVES

Published by Wildlife Education, Ltd.
12233 Thatcher Court, Poway, California 92064
contact us at: **1-800-477-5034**
e-mail us at: **animals@zoobooks.com**
visit us at: **www.zoobooks.com**

Copyright © 2003 hardbound edition by Wildlife Education, Ltd.
All rights reserved. No part of this book may be reproduced in any form without written permission from the publisher.
Printed in China

ISBN 1-932396-01-2

Wolves

Created and Written by
John Bonnett Wexo

Scientific Consultant
R. Marlin Perkins, D.Sc.
Director
WCSRC-Wolf Sanctuary

Art Credits

Page Eight and Nine: Barbara Hoopes

Page Eight: Top, Right, Bottom Right, and Bottom Left, Walter Stuart

Page Nine: Top Right and Bottom Right, Walter Stuart

Pages Twelve and Thirteen: Barbara Hoopes

Page Twelve: Bottom Left, Walter Stuart

Page Thirteen: Top Right and Bottom Right, Walter Stuart

Pages Sixteen and Seventeen: Barbara Hoopes

Page Seventeen: Right, Walter Stuart

Pages Eighteen and Nineteen: Barbara Hoopes

Page Eighteen: Middle Left, Walter Stuart

Page Nineteen: Top Right and Bottom Right, Walter Stuart

Page Twenty-two: Walter Stuart

Photographic Credits

Front Cover: © Royalty Free *(Corbis)*

Pages Six and Seven: Lynn Rogers

Pages Ten and Eleven: Background Photo, Bob & Clara Calhoun *(Bruce Coleman, Inc.)*

Page Ten: Top Right, Marty Stouffer *(Animals Animals)*; **Center Left,** Tom McHugh *(Photo Researchers)*; **Center Right,** Tom McHugh *(Photo Researchers)*; **Bottom Left,** Wayne Lankinen *(Bruce Coleman, Inc.)*

Page Eleven: Top Left, E. Hanumantha Rao *(Natural History Photo Agency)*; **Top Right,** Rick McIntyre *(Tom Stack & Associates)*

Pages Fourteen and Fifteen: Wolfgang Bayer *(Bruce Coleman, Inc.)*

Page Sixteen: Top, Patti Murray *(Animals Animals)*; **Center,** Erwin & Peggy Bauer *(Bruce Coleman, Inc.)*; **Bottom,** Leonard Lee Rue III *(After Image)*

Page Eighteen: Left, Frank Roche *(Animals Animals)*; **Right,** Lynn Rogers

Page Nineteen: Top, Jed Wilcox *(After Image)*; **Bottom,** Wolfgang Bayer *(Bruce Coleman, Inc.)*

Pages Twenty and Twenty-one: Tom McHugh *(Photo Researchers)*

Pages Twenty-two and Twenty-three: Jean-Paul Ferrero *(Ardea London)*

Back Cover: Alan & Sandy Carey

On the Cover: A Wolf

Contents

Wolves   6-7

A wolf's body   8-9

Wolves can be very different   10-11

A wolf pack   12-13

When a wolf pack hunts   16-17

Baby wolves   18-19

The future of wolves   22-23

Index   24

Wolves are the lions of the Northern Hemisphere. They are found in North America, Europe, and Asia. And in all of these places, the lives of wolves are very similar to the lives of African lions.

Like lions, wolves live in groups. Like lions, they are meat-eating animals that work together to catch their prey. And like lions, wolves are beautiful and impressive animals. In fact, some wolves even have thick ruffs of hair that look like the manes of lions.

When you consider all of these similarities, it seems strange that some people still admire lions but dislike wolves. Lions are called "lordly" and "magnificent." But a few people still think that wolves are "sneaky" and "cowardly."

This is even more of a puzzle when you find out that "man's best friend" is really a member of the wolf family. *Every single dog in the world* is descended from wolves that were tamed in the Middle East about 12,000 years ago. And most of the things that people love about dogs have been inherited from their wolf ancestors.

For example, people love the loyalty of their dogs, and this was passed on from wolves to dogs. Wild wolves can be very loyal to other wolves. People also love the friendliness and intelligence of their dogs. And these things come from wolves, too. Wild wolves in a wolf pack are often very friendly and playful with each other. And there is no doubt that wolves are among the most intelligent animals on earth.

There are many other things that we can admire about wolves. They are, for example, very adaptable animals. After humans, they are probably the most *adaptable* mammals on earth. Wolves are able to live in a wider variety of climates and habitats than most other animals—and they can survive on many different kinds of food.

There are wolves in grasslands, in forests, in swamps, and in the frozen areas of the far north. A few wolves even live in the desert. And wolves will eat *anything,* from a mouse to a moose.

The more you know about wolves, the more wonderful they seem. And perhaps this gives us a clue about the attitudes of people who dislike wolves. It may be that they don't like wolves *because they really don't know very much about wolves.* If people can love lions and dogs, then they should also be able to love wolves.

A **wolf's body** is made for chasing large prey animals and bringing them down. To do this, wolves have some excellent senses to help them find prey. They have strong muscles and long legs for running fast. And they have strong jaws and teeth for holding on to prey.

Wolves are larger than any other wild dogs and bigger than most domestic dogs. A large male wolf can be 3 feet tall and almost 6 ½ feet long. And it can weigh more than 100 pounds. Female wolves are smaller than males.

To protect them when it rains or snows, wolves have three "capes" of fur on their backs. Water runs off these capes like it runs off a raincoat. The hair in these capes may be five inches long.

Can you find the capes on the wolf below?

When wolves hunt, the colors of their fur can help them get closer to their prey without being seen. The colors of the fur may blend in with background colors in the landscape and cause a wolf to almost "disappear."

Wolves that spend a lot of time in dark forests often have dark fur.

In winter, a wolf's fur is very thick and woolly. The fur keeps the wolf warm in even the coldest weather.

In places where the plants are many different colors, the fur of wolves is often many different colors.

Wolves are fast runners. This is partly because they have long legs. Like stilts, long legs make it possible for a wolf to take longer steps as it runs.

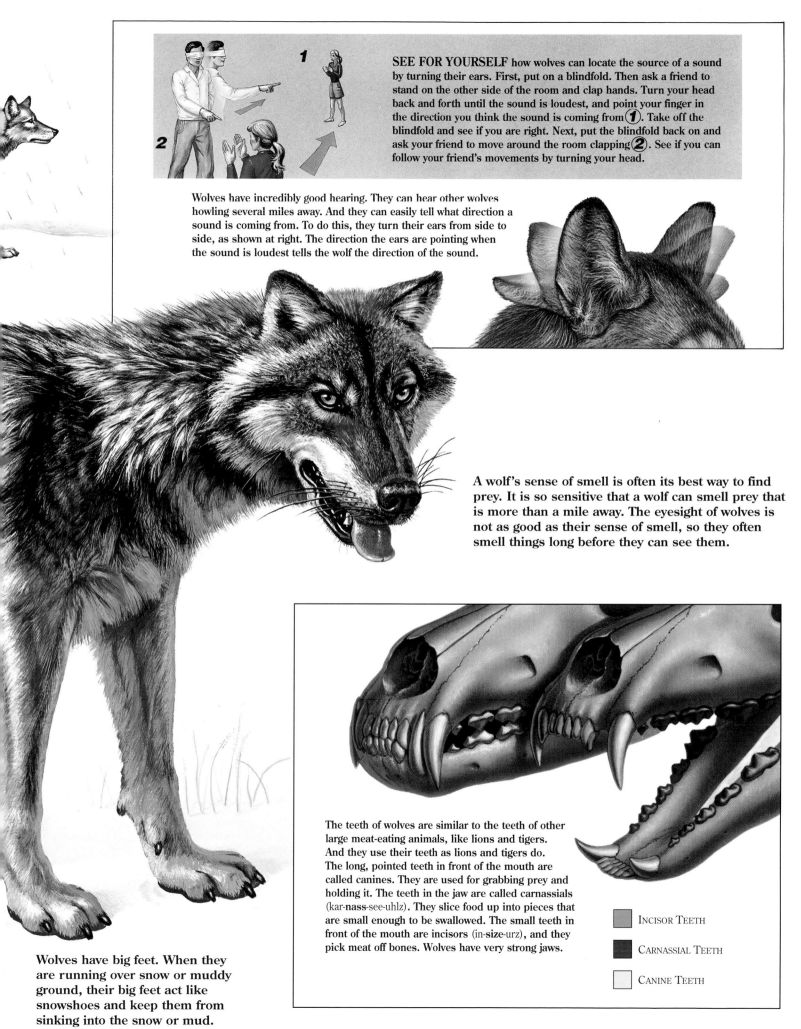

SEE FOR YOURSELF how wolves can locate the source of a sound by turning their ears. First, put on a blindfold. Then ask a friend to stand on the other side of the room and clap hands. Turn your head back and forth until the sound is loudest, and point your finger in the direction you think the sound is coming from①. Take off the blindfold and see if you are right. Next, put the blindfold back on and ask your friend to move around the room clapping②. See if you can follow your friend's movements by turning your head.

Wolves have incredibly good hearing. They can hear other wolves howling several miles away. And they can easily tell what direction a sound is coming from. To do this, they turn their ears from side to side, as shown at right. The direction the ears are pointing when the sound is loudest tells the wolf the direction of the sound.

A wolf's sense of smell is often its best way to find prey. It is so sensitive that a wolf can smell prey that is more than a mile away. The eyesight of wolves is not as good as their sense of smell, so they often smell things long before they can see them.

The teeth of wolves are similar to the teeth of other large meat-eating animals, like lions and tigers. And they use their teeth as lions and tigers do. The long, pointed teeth in front of the mouth are called canines. They are used for grabbing prey and holding it. The teeth in the jaw are called carnassials (kar-**nass**-see-uhlz). They slice food up into pieces that are small enough to be swallowed. The small teeth in front of the mouth are incisors (in-**size**-urz), and they pick meat off bones. Wolves have very strong jaws.

☐ INCISOR TEETH

■ CARNASSIAL TEETH

☐ CANINE TEETH

Wolves have big feet. When they are running over snow or muddy ground, their big feet act like snowshoes and keep them from sinking into the snow or mud.

Wolves may look very different from each other, as you can see on these pages. Some wolves are larger and more powerful than others. Some have more fur on their bodies, or thicker capes of fur on their backs. And there is an almost endless variety in the colors and patterns of fur.

In fact, when it comes to fur, every wolf seems to be different from every other wolf. And people who study wolves often use fur patterns and colors to tell one wolf from another—in the same way that you might look at human faces to tell one person from another. See if you can identify some of the differences between the wolves shown here.

A **wolf pack** is usually just a family of wolves. The members of the pack are often a mother and father wolf and their young, along with a few close relatives. The average wolf pack has seven or eight members.

The wolves in a pack are normally friendly with each other. Most of the time, they treat each other with respect. They often play together, wagging their tails and nuzzling each other.

To avoid fights among pack members there is a *dominance* (**dom**-uh-nuhnts) *order* in the pack. This means that every member of the pack has a place, or rank. Some wolves are higher in rank and some are lower. When a wolf with a higher rank has a disagreement with a wolf of lower rank, the lower-ranking wolf usually gives up without fighting.

This is very important, because wolves are such strong animals with such sharp teeth. If they didn't have a way of stopping fights before they start, they could hurt each other badly.

The leader of the pack is often the largest and strongest wolf. He is like a king. The other wolves in the pack usually do what the leader wants them to do.

Other wolves in the pack are like the nobles in a king's court. Some are more powerful and dominant than others.

Wolves at the bottom of the dominance order usually do what all of the higher-ranking wolves want them to do. They are the least powerful wolves in the pack.

Wolves howl to communicate with other members of the family. They will often howl to gather the family together before a hunt. During a hunt, howling may be used to signal the location of each wolf to other members of the family. Sometimes, wolf families seem to howl together just for the fun of it. One wolf starts howling, and the others join in.

When two wolves have a disagreement, both of them may bare their teeth and try to look as fierce as they can. The less dominant wolf usually gives up before a fight actually takes place. It rolls over on its back, and the other wolf stands over it, as shown at right.

Wolves often use their faces and ears to show other wolves how they feel. To show *anger*, a wolf may stick its ears straight up and bare its teeth①.

Suspicion is shown by pulling the ears back and squinting②. And when a wolf is *afraid*, it may flatten its ears against its head③.

1 **2** **3**

The rank of a wolf in the dominance order of the pack can often be seen in the way that it carries its tail. A more dominant wolf carries its tail high. A less dominant wolf carries it lower.

The wolves in a family pack usually cooperate in raising the young. Most adults in the pack will work to find food for the pups, and they will fight to defend the pups if necesary.

Domestic dogs behave like wolves when they accept humans as their masters. A dog sees a human as a higher-ranking dog—the leader of the pack.

13

When a wolf pack hunts, the members of the pack work together as a team. A single wolf is not large enough to hunt big animals. But a pack *combines the strength* of many wolves, and this makes it possible for them to hunt large animals.

Each family pack has a hunting territory of its own, and the pack wanders around the territory looking for prey. They sometimes travel 40 to 60 miles a day to find food. But most of the time they don't have to go that far.

Wolves are very intelligent, and they show this in the way that they choose their prey. They try to avoid prey animals that are too dangerous. When hunting large prey, they look for old or sick animals that will be easiest to catch.

Wolves hunt a wide variety of animals, and some of their prey is rather small. Beavers can be an important source of food. Some wolves hunt rabbits and squirrels. Others chase ducks, geese, and other birds. When prey is *really* hard to find, wolves may even eat mice.

When they can get it, wolves seem to prefer larger prey. They may hunt deer, elk, or mountain goats. Most of these animals are hard to catch. They can often run fast, and some of them are excellent mountain climbers.

Some animals that wolves hunt have dangerous weapons to defend themselves against attack. Deer and elk have hard hoofs that can crack a wolf's bones. Bighorn sheep can butt with their heavy horns and cripple a wolf.

Wolves don't always catch the prey they go after. In fact, many animals get away. Scientists have studied hunting wolves to see how effective they are in bringing down their prey. The scientists counted the number of moose the wolves were able to catch, and the number that got away.

Out of every 16 moose that the wolves chased, 7 got away before the wolves could even get close to them. They simply ran fast enough to keep the wolves from catching up with them. On level ground, a moose can sometimes run 35 miles per hour—as fast as a wolf. As soon as the wolves realized they weren't gaining on the moose, they gave up the chase.

7 MOOSE GOT AWAY

If a moose shows that it is willing to put up a good fight, wolves will often let it go. Two of the remaining moose turned to face the wolves when the wolves got close to them—and the wolves decided they didn't want to risk a fight.

2 MOOSE GOT AWAY

Perhaps the favorite prey of wolves is the moose. An average male moose is very large. It may weigh as much as 1200 pounds, and may stand over 6 ½ feet tall at the shoulder. The hoofs of a moose can easily kill a wolf. For this reason, wolves try to find a moose that has been weakened by sickness —or one that is bogged down in deep snow, so it cannot use its dangerous hoofs to defend itself.

All of the 7 remaining moose continued to run after the wolves caught up with them. As they ran, the moose kicked with their feet and used their antlers to keep the wolves from getting too close. All but one of these moose were able to run away from the wolves and escape.

6 MOOSE GOT AWAY

Of the original 16 moose, only one was brought down by the wolves in the end. After wolves catch their prey, they eat a lot of the meat right away. Each wolf may eat 20 pounds of meat. If there is any left, the wolves may come back later to eat it.

1 MOOSE WAS CAUGHT

Baby wolves get a lot of loving care from the moment they are born. Their mothers and fathers make sure they are well fed, kept clean, and protected constantly. In fact, wolf parents are among the best animal parents in the world.

For weeks after the pups are born, their mother stays close to them. She usually doesn't have to leave the babies to look for food, because the father and other members of the family bring food to her.

As the pups grow older and start exploring the world, other family members start playing a larger role in their lives. The young wolves learn to respect the older wolves, and they begin to find their place in the dominance order of the pack.

Wolves sometimes dig their own dens and sometimes use dens that were originally built by foxes, badgers, and other animals. When they dig their own dens, the wolves usually make more than one, so the young can be moved if one den is discovered by a predator.

About 12 days after they are born, the babies open their eyes. The eyes are blue at first, but they change to yellow and brown later on.

Wolf babies are born underground in *a den*. The den is usually dug into the side of a hill. There is a long tunnel leading to the chamber in which the babies are born. The tunnel slopes upward to prevent rain from running into the chamber.

A group of baby wolves that is born at the same time is called *a litter*. The number of babies in a litter may vary from 5 to 14. Wolf babies are blind at birth. They have fine woolly hair, and their ears are floppy. Each one of them weighs about one pound.

The pups grow very fast. By the time they are three months old, they already look like adult wolves. When they are about six months old, they start learning how to hunt.

For the first few weeks of their lives, the pups eat only the milk that they get from their mothers. After that, they start eating more and more meat. The adults carry meat back from the hunt in their stomachs. To get the meat, the pups lick the jaws of the adults. This causes the adults to bring the food back up into their mouths and give it to the pups.

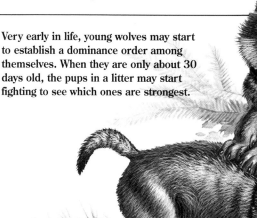

By two weeks of age, the pups can walk. A week after that, they may come out of the den for the first time and play at the entrance.

Very early in life, young wolves may start to establish a dominance order among themselves. When they are only about 30 days old, the pups in a litter may start fighting to see which ones are strongest.

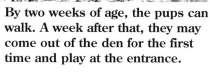

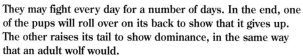

They may fight every day for a number of days. In the end, one of the pups will roll over on its back to show that it gives up. The other raises its tail to show dominance, in the same way that an adult wolf would.

Wolves that are born in the same litter may be very different in color. These two young wolves are brother and sister, but they look like they could belong in different families.

The future of wolves in the United States is looking a lot brighter today than it did in the past. Thirty years ago, there were fewer than 800 wolves left alive in the United States outside of Alaska. For hundreds of years, farmers and hunters had been killing them, and it looked as though the wolves would soon be extinct in the lower 48 states.

Then a remarkable thing happened. The Gray Wolf was listed as an *endangered species* under the Endangered Species Act, and almost immediately the number of wolves started to grow. Today, there are probably more than 3,500 wild wolves alive in the United States south of Canada—and their numbers continue to increase. The Gray Wolf is definitely back from the brink of extinction.

And this proves an important point. For almost all wild animals living in the world today, the most important factor in their survival in the future is going to be *human attitudes about animals*. In the past, almost all humans had the attitude that wolves should be shot and trapped and poisoned. But today, most people agree that wolves are unique and beautiful animals that deserve to live. And so wolves will go on living.

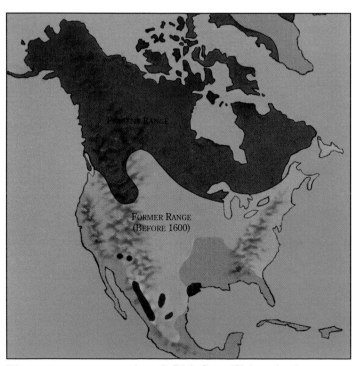

PRESENT RANGE

FORMER RANGE
(BEFORE 1600)

There are now more than 3,500 Gray Wolves in the United States south of Canada, living mostly in national parks. In addition, there are more than 6,000 in Alaska and more than 50,000 in Canada.

Index

Adaptability of wolves, 6
Anger
    displaying of, 13

Baby wolves
    See also Pups.
Beavers
    as wolf prey, 16
Big horn sheep
    as wolf prey, 16
Body, 8-9

Camouflage, 8
Canine teeth, 9
"Capes," 8
Carnassial teeth, 9
Coloring, 8

Dens, 18
Dogs
    behavior toward humans, 13
    as members of the wolf family, 6
Dominance, 12
    displays of, 13
    tail raising to show, 13, 19
Dominance order
    among pups, 18, 19

Ears
    ability to turn, 9
Extinction of wolves, 22
Eyesight, 9

Families of wolves
    See also Wolf packs.
Father wolves, 18
Fear
    displaying of, 13
Feelings
    ways of showing, 13
Feet
    size of, 9
Female wolves, 8
Fighting
    behavior during, 12
    among pups, 19
    in wolf packs, 12

Food
    amount wolves eat, 17
    for pups, 19
Friendliness of wolves, 6
Fur
    fur "capes," 8
    differences in, 10
Future of wolves, 22

Habitat, 6
Hearing, 9
Height, 8
Howling, 12
Humans
    attitudes toward wolves, 22
Hunting
    howling during, 12
    lack of success in, 17
    of large animals, 16
    territory for, 16

Incisors, 9
Intelligence of wolves, 6, 16

Jaws
    strength of, 9

Leaders
    of wolf packs, 12
Legs, 8
Litter, 18
Livestock
    killing of, 22
Loyalty
    as a wolf characteristic, 6

Male wolves
    size of, 8
Meat
    amount wolves eat, 17
Moose
    as wolf prey, 17
Mother wolves
    care of babies by, 18
Musk oxen
    as wolf prey, 16

Nose
    sensitivity of, 9
Numbers in the wild, 22

Prey
    choice of, 16
Pups
    care of, 18
    feeding of, 19
    growth rate of, 19
    raising, 13

Range, 6
    in North America, 22
Running speed, 17
Running style, 8

Senses, 8
Smell
    sense of, 9
Suspicion
    displaying of, 13

Tail raising
    to show dominance, 13, 19
Toes
    number of, 9
Types of wolves, 10

Weight
    of pups, 18
    of male wolves, 8
Winter coat, 8
Wolf packs, 6
    behavior in, 12
    hunting of large animals by, 16
Wolves
    as a danger to people, 22
    humans' dislike of, 6
    loyalty of, 6
    types of, 10